HISTORY'S YEARBOOK

GIRL INNOVATORS

VIRGINIA LOH-HAGAN

But I was free, and they should be free.
-Harriet Tubman

I am not afrai[d] I was born to d[o this.]
-Joan of Arc

I am a queen. And as long as I live, I will reign.
-Zenobia

To create one's world in any of the arts takes courage.
-Georgia O'Keeffe

[Victori]a Woodhull

A woman is like a tea bag. You can't tell how strong she is until you put her in hot water.
-Eleanor Roosevelt

The world has used me so unkindly. I fear it has made me suspicious of everyone.
-Mary Anning

Liberty!
–Inayat Khan's last word

If you hold your hand closed, nothing good can come in. The open hand is blessed, for it gives in abundance, even as it receives.
-Biddy Mason

side of the room and the guys on the other side of the room. I guess they didn't want to associate with me. But I could hold my own with them and sometimes did better.
-Mary Golda Ross

I've never been afraid in my life.
-Nancy Wake

I attribute my success to this: I never gave or took any excuse.
–Florence Nightingale

Women should be someone, and not something.
–Mary Cassatt

Well-behaved women seldom make history.
Laurel Thatcher Ulrich

Here is the day. We must welcome it with song.
–Marie Laveau

The title of Queen rang sweet to my ears.
-Catherine the Great

Contents

Introduction

We are celebrating girl **innovators**! Innovators are people who invent things. They come up with new ways to do things. They're trailblazers. Trailblazers make things happen. They do things first.

But it's not easy being a girl innovator. Many people think that women shouldn't work. Things are changing, though. What took so long?

Throughout history, women have shown that they're smart. They're creative. They're strong. The girl innovators in this book rise to the top. They paved the way for today's girl innovators.

Do you like to do things differently? Are you a problem solver? Do you see failures as opportunities to learn? If you said yes to all three, you have the qualities of an innovator!

Here's to you and all the girl innovators in our lives!

chapter 1

BEST ALL-AROUND

Florence Nightingale

> I attribute my success to this: I never gave or took any excuse.
>
> –Florence Nightingale

The "Best All-Around" award goes to Florence Nightingale. Nightingale was British. She was born in 1820. She **reformed** nursing. Reform means to improve.

Nightingale worked during a war. The hospitals were dirty. Sickness was spreading. Nightingale used science. She used **pie charts**. Pie charts are a way to show information. Nightingale showed how more soldiers died from poor conditions in hospitals than in battles.

She made changes. She cleaned hospitals. She created better services. She checked in on soldiers. She cooked special foods. She created a laundry to keep things clean. She started a library and a classroom. She wrote reports. She trained nurses. Her work saved many lives. She turned nursing into an important job.

chapter 2

MOST CREATIVE DUO

Lillian and Frank Gilbreth

We worked out a plan for the running of our house, adopting charts and a maintenance and follow-up system as is used in factories. –Lillian Gilbreth

The "Most Creative Duo" award goes to Lillian and Frank Gilbreth. Lillian had her **doctorate** in psychology. Doctorates are the top degrees in education. She was one of the first women engineers with a doctorate. Frank was a builder. Lillian met Frank in 1903. They had 12 children. They studied motions. They created new ways to make work and life easier. They had their own company.

Lillian invented shelves inside fridge doors. She improved can openers. She invented foot pedal trash cans. She invented wall light switches. She invented hoses for washing machines. She studied the proper heights for stoves and sinks.

Two of her kids wrote a book about their lives. The book is called *Cheaper by the Dozen*.

chapter 3

BEST SECRET KEEPER

Mary Golda Ross

> I was the only female in my class. I sat on one side of the room and the guys on the other side of the room. I guess they didn't want to associate with me. But I could hold my own with them and sometimes did better. –Mary Golda Ross

The "Best Secret Keeper" award goes to Mary Golda Ross. Ross was Cherokee. Cherokees are Native American people. She studied math. She studied **aerospace** engineering. Aerospace means space flight. In 1942, she worked on military planes.

She was recruited to join Skunk Works. Skunk Works was top secret. It did secret work. Ross was the only woman.

She created rules for working on spacecrafts. She created flight handbooks for space travel. Her work helped send people to outer space. Her work was secret. She wasn't allowed to tell anyone and she didn't.

chapter 4

MOST LIKELY TO THINK OUTSIDE THE BOX

Sarah E. Goode

> Racism and a strictly segregated society further encumbered female inventors of color.
>
> –Deborah Merritt (law professor at Ohio State University)

The "Most Likely to Think Outside the Box" award goes to Sarah E. Goode. Goode got a **patent** in 1885. Patents are proof of ownership of an invention. She was the first African American woman to do so.

Goode was born into slavery. She won her freedom. She moved to Chicago. She married a **carpenter**. Carpenters build things out of wood.

Goode opened a furniture store. Her customers didn't have a lot of money. They lived in small places. They didn't have a lot of room. Goode invented a folding bed for her buyers. Her bed was a desk by day. It had room to store things. It could fold down into a bed. This invention helped save room for her customers.

chapter 5

MOST TECHIE

Hedy Lamarr

> Inventions are easy for me to do. I suppose I just came from a different planet.
>
> –Hedy Lamarr

The "Most Techie" award goes to Hedy Lamarr. Lamarr was a movie star. But she was also an inventor. She's known as the mother of Wi-Fi. Wi-Fi allows us to connect to the internet without a wire.

Lamarr was born in 1913. Her mother was a pianist. Her father was a banker. Lamarr was taught to think and explore. At age 5, she took apart her music box. She liked seeing how things worked.

She made tablets that fizzed into soda when dropped in water. She helped design airplanes. She helped create a secret communications system. Her ideas led to the technology we use today.

chapter 6

MOST CARING

Helen Rodríguez-Trías

> No one is going to have quality of life unless we support everyone's quality of life.
>
> –Helen Rodríguez-Trías

The "Most Caring" award goes to Helen Rodríguez-Trías. Rodríguez-Trías fought for human rights. She was a children's doctor. She served women and children of color in poor cities.

She was Puerto Rican. She studied and worked at the University of Puerto Rico. Around 1960, she opened a center for newborn babies. This was the first of its kind in Puerto Rico. She made a lot of changes. She decreased the number of babies who died.

She also worked at a hospital in New York. She changed how hospital workers worked. She wanted them to be aware of cultural issues. She created rules to better serve women and children. She wanted everyone to have good health care.

chapter 7

MOST WELL-ROUNDED

Ruth Graves Wakefield

> We had been serving a thin butterscotch nut cookie with ice cream. Everybody seemed to love it. But I was trying to give them something different. So, I came up with Toll House cookies.
>
> –Ruth Graves Wakefield

The "Most Well-Rounded" award goes to Ruth Graves Wakefield. Wakefield did it all. She was a teacher, baker, and business owner. She even wrote a cookbook!

She owned a hotel in Massachusetts. The hotel was called the **Toll** House Inn. Tolls are fees. People used to pay tolls there. Wakefield was the cook and baker. She was famous for her desserts. She tried a different recipe. She chopped up a chocolate bar. She added chocolate bits into cookie dough.

In World War II, soldiers ate her cookies. They loved them. They wrote home asking for cookies. The cookies reminded them of home. People wrote to Wakefield for her recipe. Her cookies were a hit!

chapter 8

MOST ADVENTUROUS

Jeanne Villepreux-Power

[Jeanne Villepreux-Power is the] Mother of Aquariophily.

–Richard Owen (English scientist)

[Note: Aquariophily means the study of life in tanks.]

The "Most Adventurous" award goes to Jeanne Villepreux-Power. She was famous for inventing fish tanks. She did this in 1832.

At age 18, she walked to Paris. She walked 250 miles (402 kilometers). She wanted to be a dressmaker. She rose to the top. She sewed clothes for royal weddings. She married a rich man. She moved from France to Italy. She studied sea life. She studied octopuses holding tools. She traveled. She recorded what she saw. She collected samples. She published her work.

Villepreux-Power moved from Italy to England. She shipped her books and papers. Her work was lost. She stopped researching. But she continued to write.

chapter 9

BEST START-UP IDEA

Sarah Breedlove

> If I have accomplished anything in life, it is because I have been willing to work hard.
>
> –Sarah Breedlove

The "Best Start-Up Idea" award goes to Sarah Breedlove. A start-up is a new business. Breedlove was born in 1867.

Many African American women had problems with their hair. There weren't **products** designed for them on the market. Products are things that are sold. Breedlove wanted to change that. She made her own hair care and beauty products. She made them for black women.

She started a business. She wanted to sound fancy. So, she changed her name to Madam C. J. Walker. She opened a beauty training school. She hired salespeople. This created jobs for many black women.

Breedlove made a lot of money. She gave her money to help communities. She was the richest African American. She was a self-made millionaire.

chapter 10

TRENDSETTER

Catherine de' Medici

> Peace is carried on a stick.
>
> –Catherine de' Medici

The "Trendsetter" award goes to Catherine de' Medici. She set trends. Trends are popular fads. Others copied what she did. Medici lived in the 16th century. She was Queen of France. She came from a rich and powerful Italian family.

She brought many new ways to France. She brought cooking tools. She brought Italian styles. She brought fireworks. She brought **perfumes**. Perfumes are nice smells people wear. Medici put perfume on her gloves. They were called "sweet gloves." This became popular in France.

Medici was short. She wanted to look taller at her wedding. She wore high heels. She was the first to do so in France. She wasn't afraid to try new things.

chapter 11

BEST WRITER

Wang Zhenyi

Women are the same as men. Are you not convinced? Daughters can also be heroic.

–Wang Zhenyi

The “Best Writer” award goes to Wang Zhenyi. Zhenyi lived from 1768 to 1797.

Girls couldn’t go to school. But Zhenyi’s family were scholars. Scholars are people who study. Zhenyi read a lot of books. She taught herself many topics. She focused on math and **astronomy**. Astronomy is the study of space. Zhenyi had male students. This wasn’t done at the time.

Zhenyi wrote books. She wrote articles. She wrote about space. She even wrote about why people couldn’t fall off the earth.

Her writing was innovative for her time. She was direct. She explained things in a simple way. She wanted to make science easy for everyone. She was also a poet. She wrote about women’s rights.

chapter 12

LIFE OF THE PARTY

Ruth Handler

> We didn't know how to run a business. But we had dreams and talent.
>
> –Ruth Handler

The "Life of the Party" award goes to Ruth Handler. Handler invented the world's most popular toy. She watched her daughter play with paper dolls. So, she invented a plastic toy doll. She named the doll after her daughter. Her daughter's name was Barbara. So, the doll became known as Barbie. Handler took her invention to a toy fair. She did this in 1959. The Barbie doll became a hit. Handler also invented a male doll. The male doll was named after her son. Her son's name was Ken.

Handler also survived breast **cancer**. Cancer is a sickness. She invented a prosthetic to help survivors like her. A prosthetic is a man-made device designed to replace a body part. She helped a lot of women.

Top Memories

- **Around 370 to 415 CE:** Hypatia of Alexandria was one of the first women to study and teach math, astronomy, and philosophy. She invented a tool to measure water density. Density means thickness.
- **April 1721:** A smallpox sickness hit England. Lady Mary Wortley Montagu introduced inoculation to England. Inoculation is giving people medicine to fight sickness. Montagu saw it done in Turkey. She had her daughter inoculated. This was the first time it was done in England. People called her a bad mother. Montagu convinced others to do this. She saved millions of lives.
- **May 5, 1809:** Mary Dixon Kies was the first woman to get a U.S. patent. She invented a way to weave straw with thread. This improved hat making.
- **May 10-November 10, 1876:** The United States hosted its first world's fair. The event was in Philadelphia. Women's rights groups wanted to be included. They created a Women's Pavilion. A pavilion is a building. Over 80 women showed off their inventions.

Advice from the Field

Rose Totino's parents were Italian immigrants. Her family settled in Minneapolis. They opened a pizza restaurant in the 1950s. At that time, pizza was only popular in New York and Chicago. For the rest of America, pizza was new. But Totino helped make pizza available to all. She invented a way to freeze pizza so it still tasted good. She got a patent for her idea. She sold her business to Pillsbury in 1975. She made over $20 million from that deal. At age 60, Totino became Pillsbury's first female vice president. At age 79, she was the first woman in the Frozen Food Hall of Fame. Her advice is to focus on what you know and work hard. She said, "Never beyond my wildest dreams did I imagine we'd ever grow this big. We didn't plan on setting the world on fire. We just knew how to make good pizza."

Student Life & Clubs

Are you interested in being an innovator? Do you have a cool idea for a toy or game? Consider the Young Inventor Challenge (YIC)! This is a contest for young inventors. The contest is open to kids ages 6 to 18. It's a chance for young inventors to show off their ideas. Inventors submit a short video. They submit their inventions. The judges help young inventors. Judges include big toy companies. They include people from TV and newspapers. They include businessmen. Each inventor is given a mentor. Mentors are helpers. They help people succeed. They give feedback to make ideas better. There are two groups for judging. The junior group is ages 6-11. The senior group is ages 12-18. Prizes include Most Creative and Best Video. Ellie Skalla won in 2017. She was 11 years old when she entered. She said, "Be creative and original. Test your game many times before the contest."

> "Well-behaved women seldom make history."
>
> –Laurel Thatcher Ulrich

Did You Know...

- Many women invented things for homes. This is because they worked in homes. Josephine Cochrane invented the dishwasher, electric kettle, and ironing board.
- Many women worked in offices as secretaries. Bette Nesmith Graham invented Liquid Paper in 1956. This was used to fix typing mistakes.
- Ayla Hutchinson is from New Zealand. Her mother was chopping wood. She cut her finger. This gave Hutchinson an idea. She invented a safe wood chopper. She did this at age 13.

Learn More!

Bagieu, Penelope. *Brazen: Rebel Ladies Who Rocked the World*. New York: First Second, 2018.

Schatz, Kate, and Miriam Klein Stahl (illust). *Rad American Women A-Z: Rebels, Trailblazers, and Visionaries Who Shaped Our History ... and Our Future*. San Francisco: City Lights Books, 2015.

Thimmesh, Catherine, and Melissa Sweet (illust). *Girls Think of Everything: Stories of Ingenious Inventions by Women*. New York: Houghton Mifflin Harcourt, 2018.

Your Turn!

Now, it's your turn! You get to choose the "Top of the Class: Girl Innovator" winner. Who would you pick?

TOP OF THE CLASS: GIRL INNOVATOR

"Top of the Class" means being the best of the best. These prompts will help you think about who'd you pick for the "Top of the Class: Girl Innovator" award:

- Why is this person the best "girl innovator"? List reasons why this person deserves the award more than others.
- Think about how this person is different from girl innovators in this book. What is special about this person?
- How is this person similar to girl innovators in this book? Describe the qualities that girl innovators should have. How does this person represent those qualities?
- How does this person make the world a better place? How does this person change history? Why should we remember this person?
- Girl innovators often struggle. They may also face barriers. They're often told they can't do something. They don't run away when things get hard. How does your person overcome challenges?
- What is your person's innovation? What does it look like? What does it do? How does it improve the way things are done?
- Many girl innovators fail before they succeed. What were some mistakes this person made? How did this person fail? How did this person learn from failing?
- Innovations often lead to other innovations. What are some innovations that were inspired by this person's innovation?

Consider This!

TAKE A POSITION! Researchers say that women are less likely to get patents than men. More patents by men are approved. Why is this? Argue your point with reasons and evidence.

SAY WHAT? What is your favorite innovation? Explain the innovation. Explain why it's your favorite. Research the innovation. Who came up with it? Describe the innovator.

THINK ABOUT IT! Have you innovated anything? If not, what would you like to innovate? How does your innovation make things better? How does your innovation change the way things are done?

Glossary

aerospace (AIR-oh-spase) space flight

astronomy (uh-STRAH-nuh-mee) study of space

cancer (KAN-sur) sickness

carpenter (KAHR-puhn-tur) someone who makes things out of wood

doctorate (DAHK-tur-it) the highest degree one can get

innovators (IN-uh-vay-turz) people who invent new and better ways of doing things

patent (PAT-uhnt) proof of ownership of an invention

perfumes (PUR-fyoomz) liquids made from essential oils used to make things smell good

pie charts (PYE CHAHRTS) visuals that are circles and show information in terms of percentages, or parts of a whole

products (PRAH-duhkts) goods, items sold for money

reformed (rih-FORMD) changed for the better, improved

toll (TOHL) fee

Index

45th Parallel Press

Published in the United States of America by Cherry Lake Publishing
Ann Arbor, Michigan
www.cherrylakepublishing.com

Reading Adviser: Marla Conn, MS, Ed., Literacy specialist, Read-Ability, Inc.
Book Designer: Jen Wahi

Photo Credits:©GL Archive/Alamy Stock Photo, cover (left), 20; ©American National Red Cross, photograph collection/ Library of Congres/Reproduction No., LC-DIG-anrc-19840, cover (middle), 4; ©INTERFOTO/Alamy Stock Photo, cover (right), 16; ©George Rinhart/Corbis/Getty Images, 6; ©Pictures From History/Newscom, 8; ©Shutter Fairy/ Shutterstock, 10, 24; ©skeeze/Pixabay, 12; National Institutes of Health/Wikimedia/Public Domain, 14; ©The Picture Art Collection/Alamy Stock Photo, 18; ©lynea/Shutterstock, 22; ©Bettmann /Getty Images, 26; various art pieces throughout courtesy of Shutterstock

45th Parallel Press is an imprint of Cherry Lake Publishing.

Library of Congress Cataloging-in-Publication Data

Names: Loh-Hagan, Virginia, author.
Title: Girl innovators / by Virginia Loh-Hagan.
Description: Ann Arbor : Cherry Lake Publishing, [2019] | Series: History's yearbook | Includes bibliographical references and index.
Identifiers: LCCN 2019004192| ISBN 9781534147904 (hardcover) | ISBN 9781534149335 (pdf) | ISBN 9781534150768 (pbk.) | ISBN 9781534152199 (hosted ebook)
Subjects: LCSH: Women inventors--Juvenile literature. | Women in technology--Juvenile literature. | Technological innovations--Juvenile literature.
Classification: LCC T36 .L64 2019 | DDC 609.2/52--dc23
LC record available at https://lccn.loc.gov/2019004192

Printed in the United States of America
Corporate Graphics

About the Author:

Dr. Virginia Loh-Hagan is an author, university professor, former classroom teacher, and curriculum designer. She invents stories! She lives in San Diego with her very tall husband and very naughty dogs. To learn more about her, visit: www.virginialoh.com